WHERE DAYS BEGIN

monoku

Peter Jastermsky

This world is painted on a wild dark metal

-   **Peter Matthiessen**

"*Where Days Begin* by Peter Jastermsky unspools us into an almost incantatory world of 'wordless night[s]', allowing the reader to experience a whole gamut of emotions that range from love to loss to regret to the complete breakdown of human communication hinted at by glitches, the internet taking over, and the 'lost language of analog'. Peter's monoku are masterfully crafted and employ refreshing techniques, especially the use of the period, which delightfully furthers the exploration of the single-line format: 'leaving us to imagine . broken pencil'. Divided into four sections, the title for each is a verb in the present continuous tense—as if the poet were leading the reader by the hand and showing them his universe of complex relationships, interspersed with unobtrusive scenes from nature. Taking us through the light and the shadows, we, along with the poet, wait patiently for him to 'pomegranate'."

– Shloka Shankar, Founding Editor of *Sonic Boom* & Yavanika Press

Unspooling

incantation the edge where days begin

internet down. then. we talk.

composing ourselves a perfect circle

under a canopy stars hold their light

demimonde underbellies of shadow

prethought morning unspooling a mouth of glitches

a show of gestures descending into mime

leaving us to imagine . broken pencil

holding that thought a roll of glazed eyeballs

thunderhead some ideas just keep exploding

purple phase she learns to spell *am-e-thyst*

classroom window before the bell one last dream

school's end taking a torch to the rubric

MELTING

how many days the new lovers share scents

their eyes sawdust and spit let go

driven by senses a shard of chocolate melts poetic

feasting on their own caveats taste of crow

stages of undone questioning the statues

harsh outlook the motives of windows

nude leaning out for the songbird

leading us astray another barely spelled word

dreaming in caveman we carbon date ourselves

fumbling the years a turnstile of regret

a handful of shells family reunion

except for the grackles always fitting in

hitting the floor already he is somewhere else

SLIPPING

all week . this rain . regrets nothing

pausing the ants' holiday diatomaceous earth

smokestack orphan a testimony of brownfields

slipping on subjunctives a play for the day moon

holding their tongues the winces from unmarked graves

counting breaths a barn full of swallows

sagging trellis no one tells on the roses

A part from . no small thing

a plate of thin skin thoughts

cracked heels trouble we can't run from

brushing against you I remember hunger

in thanks stretching the haves to two hands

softening melons the way of effusive

crossing her legs not a rustle in the field

SENSING

remote sensing a problem person pierces the orbit

confirm humanity we cover for robots

smart missile not waiting to dress the salad

missing lunch empty tables sit anywhere

the *perhaps later* of sudden exhales

handsewn dreams a careful stitching of breath

midnight mirror chatting up the nose hairs

with patience I just might pomegranate

fleshing out a muted year the scatter of fortunes

broken stars we turn over the toast points

weaned on apps lost language of analog

wind tickets a ghost passenger on the metro

perfect death a *bone voyage*

alone enough the last ripe notes of soliloquy

the shape of A wordless night

ACKNOWLEDGMENTS

My grateful thanks to the editors of the following publications in which present or earlier versions of some of these poems first appeared:

B͞loo Outlier Journal, bones: a journal for the short poem, Cold Moon Journal, Failed Haiku, Frameless Sky, Heliosparrow, is/let, Sonic Boom, and Weird Laburnum